TELEVISION IN SINGAPORE

An Analysis of a Week's Viewing

by

Erhard U. Heidt

Research Notes and Discussions Paper No. 44
INSTITUTE OF SOUTHEAST ASIAN STUDIES
1984

Published by
Institute of Southeast Asian Studies
Heng Mui Keng Terrace
Pasir Panjang
Singapore 0511

All rights reserved. No part of this publication may be reproduced, stored in a retrieval system, or transmitted in any form or by any means, electronic, mechanical, photocopying, recording or otherwise, without the prior permission of the Institute of Southeast Asian Studies.

© 1984 Institute of Southeast Asian Studies

ISSN 0129-8828
ISBN 9971-902-79-6

CONTENTS

	Page
LIST OF TABLES	v
PREFACE	vii

I.	INTRODUCTION	1
	Television and the Issue of Identity	1
	Methods of Study	3

II.	PROGRAMME STRUCTURE	6
	Types of Programmes: Categories	7
	Programmes of the Week: An Overview	9
	Languages of Programmes	11
	Imported Programmes vs SBC Productions	15
	Serialization	19

III.	THE TELEVISION EXPERIENCE - CONTINUITY AND FLOW	23

APPENDICES		29
1	Distribution of Programme Types by Air-Time	30
2	Programmes of the Week: Titles	32
3.1	Programme Types in Each Language: Proportion of Total Air-Time	38
3.2	Programme Types: Proportion for Each Language	39
4	Programmes with Subtitles	40

		Page
5.1	Imported Programmes: Types and Distribution	42
5.2	Imported Programmes: Country of Origin	44
5.3	SBC Productions and Imported Programmes as a Percentage of Total Air-Time	50
5.4	SBC Productions and Imported Programmes as a Percentage of Programme Type	51
5.5	SBC Productions	52
6	Commercials	55
7.1	Programmes Telecast on Monday, 13 September 1982	56
7.2	Programmes Telecast on Tuesday, 21 September 1982	57
7.3	Programmes Telecast on Wednesday, 22 September 1982	58
7.4	Programmes Telecast on Thursday, 16 September 1982	59
7.5	Programmes Telecast on Friday, 10 September 1982	60
7.6	Programmes Telecast on Saturday, 25 September 1982	61
7.7	Programmes Telecast on Sunday, 19 September 1982	63
8.1	The Telecast Programme on Wednesday, 22 September 1982, Channel 5	65
8.2	The Telecast Programme on Wednesday, 22 September 1982, Channel 8	68

BIBLIOGRAPHY   70

LIST OF TABLES

		Page
1.	Distribution of Programme Types for the Week	10
2.	Distribution of Air-time by Language	12
3.	Language Allocation of Air-time, 1979-82	13
4.	Distribution of Subtitled Programmes by Languages	14
5.	Proportion of SBC Productions and Imported Programmes	16
6.	Number and Source of Imported Programmes	17
7.	Types of SBC Productions	17
8.	Language Distribution of SBC Productions	18
9.	Distribution of Programme Types for Each Channel	24
10.	Number of Programme Items	25

PREFACE

The analysis presented in this paper forms part of a larger study on "Television as a Symbol System: Cultural Heritage in Modern Mass Communication". The field phase of this project was conducted in 1982/83 at the Institute of Southeast Asian Studies under the Stiftung Volkswagenwerk Southeast Asia Fellowship for German Scholars. I hope to be able to finish the manuscript of the research project as a whole in 1984.

The television programmes, on which the investigation is based, were telecast in September 1982. Since the quantitative analysis has already been conducted and offers some interesting insights in itself, it was decided to make this data available as soon as possible and not wait for the final manuscript.

In order, however, to preclude a misunderstanding of the scope and aim of the study, which might arise from the publication of only part of the project data, I shall use the introduction to outline the conceptual framework and the methodological approach of the project as a whole.

My thanks are due to the Institute of Southeast Asian Studies for making this research possible through their Stiftung Volkswagenwerk Southeast Asia Fellowship and for all the technical, clerical, and personal assistance provided during my stay in Singapore.

Bielefeld   Erhard U. Heidt
May 1983

I

INTRODUCTION

Television and the Issue of Identity

It is a commonly shared belief not only among laymen but also among scholars that mass media, in particular television, have a strong impact on their audience. While most people believe that the media have a direct effect on the attitudes and behaviour of the individual, the experts have become more careful. They define the role of mass media as factors in socialization, as mediators of knowledge and world-views, and regard them as instruments of enculturation, which contribute to the shaping of a cultural identity, mainly by means of their explicit contents. Even television, however, with its apparently truthful reflection of reality is not a replica-like representation of actual society, but rather a symbolic reflection of its value structure. The iconic signs of television meet a whole range of cultural meanings, which on a higher level are integrated into a comprehensive cultural picture of the world -- a world-view. The cultural determination of television systems and programmes is often asserted, but seldom is the specific manner and manifestation of a cultural influence disclosed -- apart from a rather global juxtaposition of American and non-American (European or Third World countries) cultures. What is usually lacking are thorough analyses of the content and form of television programmes and their relation to the specific socio-cultural and socio-political context in which they appear.

A discussion of mass media in developing countries or regions almost inevitably turns to the issue of media, tradition and change, and to the role television plays in the preservation and formation (or deformation) of cultural and national identities. In Singapore, these questions are rendered even more complex since Singaporeans are faced with the problem of:

- a simultaneous identity as a member of a culture, the

centre of which is outside Singapore, and as a Singaporean, as well as

- living side by side with other Singaporeans who are supposed to have the same national identity but different cultural identities.

In a simplified manner, one might say that the cultural identity of a Singaporean has its most obvious manifestations in his language (Chinese, Malay, or Indian), while the shared national identity is founded on the English language. Hence, the typical Singaporean has been described as bicultural (Clammer 1981); this is similar, if not identical with what Chan and Evers (1973) have termed the "double identity" of the Singaporean population.

The reference to language, however, is not enough to satisfactorily answer the question: What is the substance, the uniqueness of this cultural or national identity? A number of authors have attempted to contribute an answer (for examples, Benjamin 1976; Chan and Evers 1973; Chew 1976; Clammer 1981; Hassan 1976). Most of them make reference to the composite elements "Asian/traditional" and "Western/modern", and the respective value-orientation. An appropriate description of the "Singaporeanness", not just of the Singaporean population as a whole but also of the distinct cultural subgroups, would have to identify the underlying value-structure of the modern or transitional domain as well as that of the more traditional ethnic-cultural background. Values, however, cannot be observed and analysed **per se**; they become manifest via beliefs and expectations in customs, institutions, and roles: "Values are communicated, both explicitly and implicitly, through symbolic behaviour" (Sitaram and Haapanen 1979, p. 153).

If it is true, firstly, that television in societies with a developed technological mass communication system occupies the centre of the culture, and secondly, that the problem of national and cultural identities is a central issue in multilingual and multi-ethnic Singapore, than this issue should be reflected in the programmes telecast in the Republic. Hence the research questions for the present study can be defined as:

- What are the behavioural patterns, attitudes, and value-orientations implied or explicitly communicated through the television programmes in Singapore?

- What in the television programmmes can be explained as an expression or a symbolic manifestation of cultural and national identities in Singapore?

A thorough investigation of these questions is not complete without a general discussion of basic issues such as the following:

- paradigms and results of media research,
- the social definition/construction of reality,
- national and cultural identity,
- ethnicity and cultural heritage,
- language and culture,
- Asian and Western values,
- tradition and modernization.

These issues indeed form an important part of the background and a framework for the study as a whole and will be dealt with in the final manuscript.

Methods of Study

In spite of the frequent statements on the effects of television on Singapore's society, the available literature only incidently contains data which relate to the topic of the present study. Apart from an occasional table giving a breakdown of programmes according to language, and main countries of origin, or according to gross programme categories, such as drama, education/ information, etc., there is lack of more specific data on the type and content of telecast programmmes within these gross categories. In order to obtain the data necessary for this study, a combined quantitative and qualitative approach has been chosen. A quantitative view is taken to identify the overall structure of SBC's television programmes, in particular the frequency and time allocation of programmes in different languages, programme types and topics, and imported and local items. On a second level, the view is a qualitative one. Here I will try to describe the kind of programmes that are telecast and, in particular, their content and the important ideas transmitted. The present paper, however, reports only the results of the quantitative analysis. Hence, it may suffice to shortly describe the methods used in this case.

The source to be analysed is evident: the programmes of the two channels of the only television station in Singapore, that is, the Singapore Broadcasting Corporation (SBC). Since television stations all over the world usually have a very strict programme structure, in which one day differs from the next, but in which the programmes on the same weekday over the months are very similar, it was held that each weekday should be represented. In view of the time limitations of the project, a full week also seemed to be the maximum which could be handled. Although it was not possible to select a sample which -- in the strict sense of empirical research methodology -- can be regarded as representative of Singapore's television programmes, care was taken to make the sample as typical of the average Singaporean television programme as possible:

- In considering the month of analysis, August was ruled out, since the extensive coverage of events related to the National Day for more than two weeks results in a very obvious deviation from the average programme. September, in comparison, could be considered normal.

- A "constructed week" procedure was used (cf. Jones and Carter 1959), in which a sample of seven different weekdays was selected during the period from 10 to 25 September 1982. During this period, every third day was selected.

- In order to further identify deviations from the normal programme structure, the programme schedule of each selected day was compared with the published schedule of the three other same weekdays in September 1982. The comparison was made with respect to overall structure, time allocated to the four languages, and type and content of the programmes. No major deviation was found.

During the seven selected days, all television programmes (with the exception of the special school television programmes) of both SBC's channels were video-recorded. In this way, they were available for easy replay and reference.

For the purpose of this study, it is apparently easy to define the unit of analysis as "a programme item as it is produced, announced and hence generally perceived as a reference label by the audience"; and the first analysis indeed concentrates on units according to this definition. The matter, however, becomes more complex with the introduction of the concept of "television as flow" as put forward by Williams (1974), since this involves a shift from recording units to context units (Holsti 1969). While in all other media and communication systems before the advent of broadcasting, the essential items were discrete (they were offered as a sequence of specific events), the television experience of today is one of flow. This explains why the viewer tends to stay with whatever channel he began to watch (this recognition has direct consequence for programming, in particular for advertising policies), and why it is so difficult for many viewers to switch their television sets off. Media research to date has hardly been influenced by this concept, which does not regard the published sequence of discrete programme units as the most important characteristic, but rather the sequence transformed by the inclusion of another kind of sequence (first by the broadcasters and then by the viewers). A research approach which breaks the central television experience of flow back into discrete programme units, and studies only these units, leaves out of consideration a factor with important effects on the audience and thus misses an essential characteristic of a specific television system. A study which takes the concept of flow into account has to proceed on different levels of analysis, which, of course, has to consider the declared programme units and their subunits but which attempts, in addition, to identify and describe their relation and interrelation in the flux of a particular evening's programme. An attempt in such an analysis is included in this paper.

II

PROGRAMME STRUCTURE

The following quantitative analysis and description is based on the recording of seven weekdays. It describes the programmes as they have been really telecast and deviates slightly from the printed programme schedules, since it takes into account those changes which occur without prior announcements.

The tables in the Appendices which break down the total air-time into time-slots allocated to different languages, programme types, and so forth, do not take into account those "hidden" programme types which are never published, although they are telecast each day and take up a considerable amount of air-time. They comprise commercials, internal publicity of the television station, national policy messages, and presentation of national symbols. Taking these programmes statistically correct into account would have required an enormous time-taking effort, since these programmes, in particular the commercials, are quite unevenly distributed, so that some popular dramas are surrounded and interrupted up to five times by over forty advertisements, while other programmes are not affected at all. Time for these programme types has been taken cumulatively but, nevertheless, carefully. The exact timing of these short items (often less than 20 seconds), however, is prone to marginal errors. In addition, the necessary change of cassettes was made on four days during a commercial interval between programmes; the missing data have been averaged from the remaining three days.

Figures, which as a whole are taken as approximating the average television week in Singapore, have been rounded so as to add up to 100%. Hence, small differences in quantitative value should not be taken as a basis for far-reaching conclusions. None of the findings of this study will be based on small nominal differences.

Type of Programmes: Categories

The categories used to describe the different types of television programmes are not fully mutually exclusive. It is not always easy to separate one category from another. The ensuing difficulties in unambiguously describing actual television programmes by means of these categories is enhanced by the fact that an individual programme may contain elements which fall into different categories. In such a case, the category which either describes the main focus of the programme or the terms in which it is planned, presented and hence generally perceived by the audience has been used. In the following descriptions an effort has been made to identify potential cases of ambiguity and to indicate relations and distinctions between the categories.

The following listing of programme types does not constitute an order of priority or importance attached to the different types of programmes. The categories are grouped in such a way that those numbered 1 to 5 may be described as having their main focus on information transmission, that is, after watching these programmes the viewer should have acquired additional knowledge or formed an opinion about an issue. In contrast, categories numbered 6 to 10 have their main focus on what is traditionally labelled "entertainment", that is, the main interest and the fun is supposed to be derived from the act of watching: it would not matter very much if one could not remember the informational content of these programmes the next morning. Categories numbered 11 to 14 refer to "hidden" programme items which as a rule are not printed in any television schedule, but which are nevertheless telecast every day, occupy a considerable amount of air-time, and often give a distinct colouring to an evening's telecast.

1. <u>News</u>. This category is reserved for news bulletins which are labelled accordingly in the programme print-out.

2. <u>Documentary/Feature/Magazine</u>. Programme items under this category give, mainly and essentially, a direct presentation of the substance of an issue. This category is subdivided according to topical focus into culture and arts, current affairs, history, magazine, nature, and science.

3. <u>Opinion/Discussion</u>. This category refers to specially arranged items of argument and discussion. The formation of opinion or the clarification of an issue is, however, not achieved by a direct presentation of the issue in question as in "Documentary" but by an exchange of arguments and opinions about it.

4. Education. This category refers to non-formal programmes for self-improvement, mainly by teaching specific skills in the field of crafts and hobbies. It does not include the formal course programmes for schools which are telecast on selected weekdays between 11.20 a.m. and 3 p.m. These programmes are apparently not intended for even incidental viewing by the general public, since their schedule is neither printed in the weekly television supplement of the popular daily newspapers nor in the **Radio and TV Times,** published by SBC itself.

5. Local Information. Items under this category give information about local events and happenings as well as advice and suggestions about activities in Singapore. This category, however, does not include commercial advertising programmes nor announcements about television programmes themselves; these items will be dealt with under separate headings.

6. Children's Programme. This category refers to those programmes which are specifically produced and presented for children. Although children will usually watch other programmes as well, items in this category are explicitly presently to that target audience. This category has the subdivisions of drama/narration and educational/informational programmes. Both these subdivisions overlap with other programme types. Their listing under "Children's Programme", however, seems to be justified since firstly they are **children's** programmes, and secondly, the educational programmes such as "Sesame Street", "The Electric Company", "3-2-1 Contact", and so forth, often conceal their educational and instructional intentions under an entertaining cover of cartoons, puppets and other dramatic devices. In constrast to all other programme categories in this list, "Children's Programme" does not refer to a type of content but to an intended audience target group. It is nevertheless relevant as a category, since it is used by producers and viewers alike. The subcategories, then, refer to the type of content - paralleling or repeating the categories of non-children programmes.

7. Drama. Items under this category include plays in the traditional sense, that is, they translate a story, a plot into dramatic presentation. This category is subdivided, using the conventional labels "adventure" (including detective drama), and "family" (including comedy).

8. <u>Sports</u>. This is defined as televised sports events or reports of such events.

9. <u>Music</u>. This category refers to programmes in the traditional concert-hall style, in the sense that they are essentially straight-forward presentations of musical pieces from a mainly classical (European or Asian) repertoire.

10. <u>Show</u>. This category contains the rest -- very often taking up a considerable amount of programme time -- of what is conventionally conceived as "light entertainment programmes". Its two subdivisions are musical shows, and games and quiz programmes. The musical show differs from the "Music" programmes in that it emphasizes the **show** character of the presentation and is often interspersed by other items, such as comedy, so that the dividing line to a variety show is difficult to draw. In this study, a variety show is treated as a variation of a musical show.

11. <u>Commercial</u>. This category comprises all advertising programmes with the exception of SBC internal publicity items, and national policy messages.

12. <u>National Policy Message</u>. This category refers to programmes telecast on behalf of government or government-related authorities with information about the direction of national and societal politics, such as speeches by government representatives, or with appeals to mobilize the audience for national development, for desired activities or changes in behaviour, such as national campaigns.

13. <u>Publicity (Television Internal)</u>. This includes the presentation of programme information with respect to SBC's television programmes through previews, advance announcements, and so forth.

14. <u>National Symbols</u>. Items in this category consist of presentations of such items as the National Anthem, the national flag, or other approved or conventional national symbols.

Programmes of the Week: An Overview

Television transmission hours in the recorded week total 115:40 hours. Of this total air-time 72:50 hours, or 63% of transmission time, are transmitted on Channel 5, while the figures for Channel 8 are 42:50 hours, or 37%. Hidden in the total transmission time are the unannounced programme items of commercials (8:22 hours), SBC internal publicity (1:57 hours), and national symbols (1:02 hours), which together amount to 11:21 hours, or 9.8% (that is, as much as "News") of transmission time. Leaving these unannounced items out of consideration, the total number of programmes telecast in the recorded week is 203. This number, however, includes the two programme items, "Your Shopping Guide" (one in English, one in Chinese), which present only sequences of SBC-produced commercials, and hence are elsewhere in this study included in the category "Commercial".

A listing of these programmes according to type reveals that by far the largest group in terms of air-time allocated to it is (adult) drama, followed by children's programmes, and shows.

TABLE 1
Distribution of Programme Types for the Week

	Programme Type	Number of Programme Items	Percentage of Total Air-Time
1	Drama	53	44.8
2	Children's Programme	44	14.3
3	Show	14	11.6
4	Documentary	29	10.7
5	News	35	9.6
6	Sports	5	3.2
7	Opinion	4	2.9
8	Education	6	1.6
9	Local Information	6	0.7
10	Music	5	0.4

A more detailed breakdown, according to further sub-categories and to language used, is given in Appendix 1. In order to show what kind of programmes are included under each category, Appendix 2 presents the full list of the programme titles.

Languages of Programmes

The recorded week approximates as closely as possible the average television week in Singapore. The figures for the following comparison and check over four weeks in September and October 1982 are taken from **Sunday Nation** and **Sunday Times**, as these are more up-to-date (compared with **Radio and TV Times**) and take into account some of the apparently unavoidable programme changes.

For the period 6 September to 3 October 1982, total television transmission time amounted to 473:15 hours, of which 279:20 hours were in English, 130:05 hours in Chinese, 34:10 hours in Malay, and 29:10 hours in Tamil/Hindi. The Muslim festival of Hari Raya Haji, a public holiday, on Tuesday, 28 September 1982, accounts for the following increases in the different language programmes: English 5 hours, Chinese 1:40 hours, and Malay 3:20 hours. The average week for this period, when corrected for these Hari Raya distortions, has the following distribution:

Total Air-Time	:	115:48 hrs	=	100.0%
English	:	68:34	=	59.2
Chinese	:	32:06	=	27.7
Malay	:	7:43	=	6.7
Tamil	:	7:25	=	6.4

The data for our recorded constructed week show that it very closely resembles the average week:

Total Air-Time	:	115:40 hrs	=	100.0%
English	:	69:40	=	60.2
Chinese	:	31:35	=	27.3
Malay	:	7:00	=	6.1
Tamil	:	7:25	=	6.4

Of the total air-time, 72:50 hours, or 63% are transmitted via Channel 5, and 42:50 hours, or 37%, via Channel 8. The different language programmes distributed between the two channels are shown in Table 2.

TABLE 2
Distribution of Air-time by Language

	Channel 5	Channel 8
English	59:20	10:20
Chinese	6:05	25:30
Malay	7:00	–
Tamil	0:25	7:00
Total	72:50 hrs	42:50 hrs

The figures show that, although the programmes are telecast in the four official languages, the distribution of air-time to the various languages is quite uneven and does in no way relate to any census data about language distribution among Singapore's population. SBC officals, when asked about the criteria for allocating the proportion of air-time to the four languages, referred to "historical reasons". Further questioning revealed that this pattern apparently just evolved over time, and that, if a deliberate decision was taken in the beginning, broadcasters today are no longer aware of the reason. There was no indication that SBC intends to change the present allocation pattern. In particular, I was unable to find any corroboration for the statement that "the desired proportion has been set at 35% for English, 35% for Chinese, 20% for Malay, and 10% for Tamil" (Chen and Kuo 1978, p. 4). A comparison of language allocations over the past three years shows no development in this direction. If anything, it reveals a slight tendency towards increasing the time allocation of Chinese programmes at the expense of English ones, but definitely no similar increase for those in Malay and Tamil (Table 3)*.

---

*   Data are taken from Ow (1979); **SBC Annual Report 1981/82**; and my own recordings.

TABLE 3
Language Allocation of Air-time, 1979-82
(in %)

	English	Chinese	Malay	Tamil
1979	62.7	23.6	7.5	6.2
1981/82	61.0	26.1	6.6	6.3
September 1982	60.2	27.3	6.1	6.4

This finding is in line with a policy statement by Ong Teng Cheong, then Minister for Communications, Acting Minister for Culture and Chairman of SBC. When asked, on the occasion of the conversion of RTS (Radio and Television Singapore) to SBC, whether there would be any changes in the present policy on air-time accorded to the four languages, he declared: "As I said in Parliament during the final reading of the SBC Bill, the quantum of air-time that the minority community are having now on television will not be reduced though there may be adjustments to improve presentation and quality" (**The Mirror**, No. 5, 1980). This assurance was repeated by the then General Manager, and now Deputy Chairman, of SBC (Cheng Tong Fatt, 1980).

If one takes a look at the percentage of total air-time allocated to the programme types in the different languages, one finds that the list is topped by English drama (24.1%), followed by Chinese drama (17.1%), English children's programmes (11.4%), English documentaries (8.3%), and English shows (5.6%). All other programme types score less than 4% (Appendix 3.1). A comparison of programme types across the four languages reveals a quite uneven distribution (Appendix 3.2). In the English language section, the three programme types with the largest share of air-time are drama (40.1%), children's programmes (19%), and documentaries (13.8%). Among the Chinese programmes, the list is topped by drama (62.5%), followed by shows (14.2%), and news (7.1%). The sequence for Malay is news (33.3%), shows (21.4%), and drama (19%); and for Tamil, it is drama (38.2%), news (31.5%), and shows (12.4%). The total transmission time allocated to Malay and Tamil language programmes, however, is too short to base far-reaching conclusions on small differences in transmission time for a particular programme type. Considering that, in general, television is mainly watched for entertainment, what can be said is that, in comparison to English and Chinese programmes, the two minority language programmes are over-weighted with news and documentaries, which have no cultural connection with those specific language groups. Among the Malay as well as the Tamil programmes, 2:45 hours (equalling 39.3% and 37.1% respectively) are taken up by such informational items. This leaves 4:15 hours and 4:40 hours of the Malay and Tamil transmission time respectively, for all other programme types during the week. Although survey data show "that there is a very high correlation between the ethnic background of the audience and the language of TV programmes they watch" (Chen and Kuo 1978, p. 9), it is quite obvious that the Malay and Indian communities in particular have to turn to other language programmes for entertainment (and further information). This assumption can be corroborated by audience data collected by Survey Research Singapore (SRS) for 1982. According to this survey, more than 50% of the Malay and Indian population (like all other Singaporeans) watch television every day or almost every day. Both groups turn out to be heavy viewers. Slightly over 50% of the Malays and almost as high a percentage of the Indians watch television from two to five hours daily. This figure is considerably higher than the Singaporean average of about 26% of viewers in that group. In most cases, the additional programmes chosen will be in English. The SRS data also show that, of necessity, in comparison to the Chinese audience, a much higher percentage of the Malay and Indian viewers watch English-language programmes.

The language allocation pattern is somewhat changed through the use of subtitles. The distribution of subtitles is, again, uneven, and it is also not the case, as has been claimed, that "as a principle, non-English programmes are supplied with English subtitles" (Chen and Kuo 1978, p. 10). In terms of transmission time, slightly less than one-third of the programmes makes use of subtitles. Table 4 gives a breakdown for the various languages.

TABLE 4
Distribution of Subtitled Programmes by Languages

Programme Language	Total Air-time (Hrs:Min)	Subtitles in Each Language (Hrs:Min)	As % of Programmes In Each Language	As % of Total Air-time
English	69:40	12:30	17.9	10.8
Chinese	31:35	19:10	60.7	16.6
Malay	7:00	1:45	25.0	1.5
Tamil	7:25	3:15	43.8	2.8
Total	115:40	36:40		31.7

A look at the list of programmes telecast during the recorded week (Appendix 4) shows that of the 36:40 hours of subtitled programmes, 33:40 hours, or 91.8%, fall into the category of "drama", while 2:45 hours, or 7.5%, are documentaries. It also reveals the pattern that, with only one exception, all Chinese drama serials are subtitled in English, and that the English drama telecast each day during prime time on Channel 5 is subtitled in Malay. Hence, although subtitles are as a rule not announced in the printed programme schedules, television viewers know by now when to expect subtitles and when not.

Although subtitles are a useful means to make programmes accessible to other language groups, there are certain shortcomings. More often than not, the subtitles are not direct translations of the dialogue, but only summarize what is said. Thus, the viewer from another language group is able to follow the action and get a rough idea, but misses the finer points of the dialogue. In addition, the subtitles, in particular those provided by the original producer and not subsequently by SBC, are often hardly legible. SBC recognizes this fact by flashing -- as an apology -- the information onto the screen that "subtitles are provided by the producer".

Imported Programmes vs SBC Productions

Much has been said and written about the detrimental and alienating effects of imported programmes (in particular those from the West) on Singapore's society. The use made in the following analysis of the terms "Asian" and "Western", is -- in contrast to most of these statements -- purely descriptive and not meant as an explanation for anything.

During the recorded week, the relation of SBC productions to imported programmes shows that there has been no significant change over several years. Although a number of writers have given the ratio of SBC productions to imported programmes as 40:60, available data since the mid-seventies show that local productions never contributed more than one-third of the total transmission time, and that for 1979-81 they were well below 30%. The **SBC Annual Report 1981/82** gives a higher percentage (almost 30%) for SBC productions. This, however, does not reflect a change in policy or production; the same programmes are only categorized in a different way. The difference between the data presented here and those of SBC stems from the classification of dubbed programmes. In the latest report, all programmes dubbed by SBC are counted as "SBC produced", while I think there is good reason to classify them under "imported programmes".

TABLE 5
Proportion of SBC Productions and Imported Programmes

	Number of Programmes	Air-time	Percentage of Total Air-time
SBC Productions	72	31:25 hrs	27.1
Imported Programmes	131	84:15 hrs	72.9
Total	203	115:40 hrs	100.0

Of the imported programmes, 101, equalling 58:50 hours or 50.9% of air-time, are of Western origin, while 30 programmes, equalling 25:25 hours, or 22.0% of total air-time, stem from Asian countries. The categorization of programmes as Western or Asian according to their country of origin -- and the implicit assumption that Western productions present Western topics, values and world-views, while Asian programmes deal with Asian topics, and so forth -- has to be qualified by a closer look at the content, since sometimes the opposite is the case. The U.S. production "Erica", for example, attempts to teach the appreciation of Japanese and Chinese art forms. The Japanese programme "Heidi", on the other hand, is based on the Swiss novel, while "World Famous Fairy Tale", which is also imported from Japan, tells a story about slavery problems in nineteenth-century USA. Appendix 5.1 and 5.2 provide a comprehensive breakdown of imported programmes according to country of origin, type of programme, and title of individual items.

The list of countries from which programmes are imported is topped by the United States, followed by Hong Kong, which has only a marginal advantage over Great Britain (see Table 6). However, the figures given should not be used as a basis for conclusions about the potential influence of imported programmes on Singapore society. Even if a higher percentage of programmes is imported, it does not mean that there is a free market for an uncontrolled influx of programmes and ideas. Apart from the fact that the country of origin does not reveal anything about the content, or ideas conveyed in a programme, SBC officials have repeatedly stressed that programmes telecast are, firstly, carefully selected and, secondly, censored and cut, if it is considered necessary. Dubbing and the introduction of subtitles provide an additional means of control.

Appendix 5.3 and 5.4 compare SBC productions and imported programmes according to the type. They show that, in terms of transmission time, most SBC productions are news programmes, followed by shows.

TABLE 6
Number and Source of Imported Programmes

	Country	Number of Programme Items	Percentage of Total Air-time
1	USA	70	35.9
2	Hong Kong	10	10.6
3	United Kingdom	17	10.1
4	Taiwan	6	5.1
5	Japan	11	4.0
6	India	2	2.0
7	Germany	5	1.7
8	Canada	4	1.3
9	Australia	3	0.9
10	Spain	1	0.8
11	Brunei	1	0.4
12	Netherlands	1	0.1

TABLE 7
Types of SBC Productions

	Programme Type	Number of SBC Produced Items	Percentage of SBC Production Time
1	News	35	35.3
2	Shows	8	22.3
3	Opinion	4	10.6
4	Documentary	5	9.5
5	Children's programmes	7	7.7

In other words, all news, opinion, and local information programmes as well as half of the shows are locally produced, while all educational programmes as well as the vast majority of drama, documentary and children's programmes are imported. A full list of all SBC programmes is given in Appendix 5.5.

There is wide agreement in Singapore that SBC should increase its output of locally produced programmes and change the present ratio, which is 70:30 in favour of imported programmes. In 1980, the General Manager, and now Deputy Chairman, of SBC explained: "The ultimate target is to produce 50% of SBC's television output locally" (Cheng Tong Fatt, 1980, p. 9), while recently SBC's newly appointed Director (TV Drama) announced: "SBC is working towards producing 80% of the programmes it broadcasts" (**Straits Times**, 7 March 1983). Up to September 1982, however, these plans have not been reflected in SBC's programme schedule.

Despite the assumption by even the better informed Singaporeans that local programme production "is divided equally among the four languages" (Koh 1980, p. 303), language distribution of SBC productions is as uneven as the language distribution of television programmes in general, as shown in Table 8.

TABLE 8
Language Distribution of SBC Productions

Language	:	Air-time	:	% of SBC Production
English	:	11:50 hrs	:	37.7
Chinese	:	8:45 hrs	:	27.9
Malay	:	6:10 hrs	:	19.6
Tamil	:	4:40 hrs	:	14.8
Total	:	31.25 hrs	:	100.0

On the average, the percentage of Chinese productions over the years is expected to be higher because of SBC's Mandarin drama productions. Considering that, in 1982, an average of about two hours of Chinese dramas are produced a month, this would increase the Chinese share to about 30%.

To put it again in another way, SBC produces 17% of all programmes telecast in English; while the percentages for the other languages are: Chinese 27.7%, Malay, 88.1%, and Tamil 62.9%.

Serialization

As in most other countries, the programme structure of television in Singapore is well defined and, to a large degree, predetermined. There is hardly any time-slot within each day that the experienced television viewer would not be able -- without consulting the printed programme schedule -- to tell what kind of programme will be telecast.

On the most general level, time-slots are defined in terms of generic categories, such as:

- News (each day at exactly the same time for the different languages)

- World of Sports, or

- Indian or Chinese or Midnight Movie.

Each item filling these generic categories, however, has no connection, no story-line, linking it with the preceding or the subsequent item in the same category. The structural definition on this level is similar to that of a newspaper, where the same type of content is found infallibly each day on the same page, often even on the same part of that page.

Television broadcasters have gone a step, or rather a number of steps, further in order to give continuity to their programmes. In this way, they hope to develop a reliable regular audience for their channel or station -- a feature which may become a survival factor, when the channel is partly or wholly commercialized and hence has to depend on its attraction to advertisers. This has led to a "serialization" of television programmes to such a degree that one might even call it the main structural characteristic of the television medium.

If we define a series as "a sequence of programmes which is telecast usually on the same weekday at roughly the same time in regular intervals, with at least five instalments or episodes, and which is announced under a series title (often followed by a more specific title for the individual programme item) other than the generic category described above", then it is possible to distinguish at least four main types in order of increasing coherence. The following examples are taken from the week under analysis.

    1. A series which has a common topic and which is often associated with a specific presenter or host, but in which the individual programme items have only a random connection with each other. Series of this kind are

found among most programme types. For example,

- Documentaries: "Thacker's World"; "Walter Cronkite's Universe";

- Education: "Exercise with Gloria"; "Serikandi";

- Children's Programme: "Kebekio in the Land of I Want"; "The Book Bird";

- Drama: "Cosmopolitan Theatre"; "The Wonderful World of Disney";

- Music: "World Music Album";

- Shows: almost all programmes.

2. A series in which each programme is apparently self-contained, but which has a hidden intentional link (at least in the mind of the planners and producers), so that the sum total is supposed to be more than just the addition of isolated bits. They are intended to give the viewer a more complete picture of a topic or help him acquire more complex abilities. Hence, these series are mainly found among programmes with a strong informational or educational focus. For example,

- Documentaries: "Age of Uncertainty"; "Air";

- Education: "Skills of Defensive Driving";

- Children's Programme: "Sesame Street"; "The Electric Company".

The programme type with which serialization is most commonly associated, however, is drama. Here, a distinction is sometimes made between a "series" and a "serial", which somehow parallels the distinction between the two types just described.

3. A drama series which is characterized by a continuity of main character or characters, time and place, or environment. Each episode is usually a self-contained programme, following the same pattern with little or no opportunity for the development of the main character. Most Western drama series come under this category. Examples are:

- Adventure: "Magnum"; "Supertrain"; "Target"; "The Wild Wild West";

- Family and Social: "Father Murphy"; "Harper Valley, PTA"; "Laverne and Shirley"; "Mr Merlin";

- Children's Programme: "Maggie's Moor"; "Secret Valley".

4. A drama serial which, in addition to the feature of a series, has a continuity of action, that is, the story develops over several subsequent episodes. It has been pointed out that this type has a precedent in eighteenth and nineteenth-century serialized fiction (Williams 1974, p. 60). Most Chinese drama as well as about half of the children's drama programmes belong to this category. Examples are:

- Adventure: "The Chivalrous Pugilist"; "On the Waterfront";

- Family and Social: "A House Is Not A Home"; "The Jaws";

- Children's Programme: "A Little Silver Trumpet"; "The Ravelled Thread".

The first two types of series together comprise 54 programmes taking up 24.9% of overall transmission time, while the third and fourth types together comprise 58 programmes taking up 37.3% of total air-time. Thus, out of 201 programmes, 112 items, equalling 70:55 hours or 62.2% of total air-time, can be categorized under a series title other than the generic type category, and hence are series according to my definition. This does not taken into account the **ad hoc** series such as the Confucian philosophy lectures given by visiting scholars or the telecast of "Debate '82". If one includes these programmes as well as "News", "Cultural Diary", "World of Sports", "Thursday Night Entertainment Special", and so forth, then more than 80% of transmission time has a pre-defined content, which remains unchanged over weeks, months, or even years.

This all-pervasive feature of serialization is not just interesting as a fact in itself, it is also of relevance for the discussion of the social function and potential effects of television. In line with the theoretical paradigm of "habitualization through long-time exposure", which media effects studies have indicated to be the most plausible, one might argue that if any influence of television programmes on viewers' expectations, world-views, value structure, and so forth, is to be assumed, or if any type of programme can be expected to reflect a society's world-views, and so forth, then it should be the series with their continuous repetition of the same basic message and pattern. One might regard this assumption at least as partly corroborated by the SRS audience data, which point at a close match, in this respect, of viewer taste and telecast series: drama serials and show series (5 and 3 items respectively) make up the majority of Singapore's top ten popular programmes during August and September 1982 (and this has virtually been the case at least during the preceding two years).

The high degree of serialization is another reason that the programme structure each week resembles that of another so closely, and there is so little room for variation that almost any week (apart from those with special events) may be considered as "average" and "typical".

III

THE TELEVISION EXPERIENCE - CONTINUITY AND FLOW

Before the advent of video recorders -- and that is an issue beyond the scope of this paper -- viewers did not watch television programmes of the same type grouped together nor did they switch on the television set for a single item and then switch it off after the item had been telecast. When viewing television broadcasts, the normal pattern was and still is to watch several subsequent programmes over a longer period of time. In order to come closer to the actual experience of televiewing, I shall now look at the composition of the larger programme unit, that is, the distribution of programme types

- for each channel over the week,

- for the English and Chinese language programmes over the week, and

- for an evening's telecast.

The objective is to find out whether it is possible to identify and describe specific distinctive patterns for any or each of these categories.

An analysis of the distribution of programme types for each channel separately shows that there is a high degree of similarity. The five most frequent programme types, which on both channels account for roughly 90% of total air-time, are allocated comparable time-slots.

Consequently, the deviation from the distribution pattern for both channels, as given in Appendix 1, is even less.

The picture changes somewhat if one looks separately at the English and Chinese language programmes and also takes into account the number of programme items. The decision to leave the

TABLE 9
Distribution of Programme Types for Each Channel

Programme Type	Percentage of Air-Time in	
	Channel 5	Channel 8
Drama	46.1	42.6
Children's Programme	13.0	16.5
Shows	11.1	12.6
Documentary	10.7	10.5
News	8.8	10.9
	89.7	93.1

Malay and Tamil programmes out of consideration here seems justifiable, since, because of their restricted transmission time and the ensuing restrictions on programme types telecast (cf. Appendix 3.2), both cannot be considered as representing self-contained and (more or less) complete programme schedules in their own right. They depend on items from other language "streams" as complements. The assumption that Chinese programmes have a large audience which treats this language section like a channel in its own right and watches Chinese programmes almost exclusively can be supported by audience data from Survey Research Singapore. In contrast to the other ethnic groups, there is for the Chinese population a large difference in number between those who watch Chinese programmes (91%) and those who watch Chinese plus English programmes (57%).

In addition to the hours of transmission for each programme type, the number of programme items is also relevant. If for the same air-time, one programme type has a greater number of short items, which are distributed over a longer period, this means that these items appear more often and hence stand a greater chance of being seen by a larger number of viewers. To give an example from the recorded week: while, in terms of air-time, the chances of viewing an English language documentary compared to an English language show are 3:2, in reality the chances are much higher. Since three or four documentaries are telecast each day compared to less than one show, the chances in favour of documentaries -- in terms of programme items -- would be 4:1.

Since transmission time in English amounts to more than double that in Chinese, it is not surprising that, in terms of air-time and the number of items, English language items

TABLE 10
Number of Programme Items

Programme Type	English	Chinese	Malay	Tamil	Total
News	14	7	7	7	35
Documentary	23.5*	2.5*	2	1	29
Opinion	3	1	-	-	4
Education	5	-	1	-	6
Local Information	3	3	-	-	6
Children's Programmes	36	5	1	2	44
Drama	30	18	2	3	53
Sports	5	-	-	-	5
Music	1	3	-	1	5
Show	6	5	2	1	14
	126.5	44.5	15	15	201

* The 0.5 programme items occur because the bilingual programme "Musical Soiree" is counted as half for each language.

constitute the majority of programmes for each type. Taking the above figure and Appendix 3.2 together, however, one can see that the English language programmes have a disproportionately greater share of informational/educational programmes (comprising categories 1 to 5 of my programme types) and of children's programmes not only in terms of absolute air-time, but also with respect to percentage in that language and the number of programme items. The breakdown is as follows:

- Information: 18:00 hrs = 25.9%, with 48.5 items;

- Children's programmes: 13:15 hrs = 19.0%, with 36 items.

For the Chinese language programmes the figures are:

Information: 4:50 hrs = 15.4%, with 13.5 items;

- Children's programmes: 2:05 hrs = 6.6%, with 5 items.

For entertainment (drama plus show), the situation is different. While the proportion of items to transmission time is the same for both languages, the percentage of air-time is strikingly different:

- Drama (E): 34:30 hrs = 49.5%, with 36 items;

- Drama (C): 24:15 hrs = 76.7%, with 23 items.

This uneven distribution seems to point at different conceptions of public interest and of needs for information and entertainment. Although I do not think it possible to express a satisfactory balance between information, education, and entertainment in quantitative terms (definitely not 1:1:1) -- and bearing in mind the problem of using the term "entertainment" without any qualitative connotations -- one has to admit that the Chinese language programmes, if treated as a "quasi channel", has by far the highest share of entertainment programmes compared to the other three language sections. The reason for this is most likely a very pragmatic one: documentaries and educational programmes in English are not only more easily available but also less expensive to purchase. Bearing in mind, however, the popularly held belief in Singapore about the relation of language to culture and modernization, one might feel inclined to explain this finding in the framework of these assumptions.

In the Malay and Tamil sections there are 15 programmes each for the full week. This means that on each day -- apart from the news -- only one programme item (usually of a more entertaining kind) is telecast.

Useful as this analysis of programming patterns may be, if one intends to come closer to the actual television experience, one has "to go beyond the static concept of 'distribution' to the mobile conception of 'flow'" (Williams 1974, p. 78).

What is released and published as a programme schedule still has the form of a sequence of discrete and exactly defined units (cf. Appendices 7.1 - 7.7), each of which, apparently, can be individually selected for viewing. The normal behaviour of a viewer and hence his television experience, however, is different: he automatically switches on the TV set when he comes home; and when you ask him what he is doing, he will most likely tell you that he is "watching television" and not give a specific programme. The use of the generic media category to describe his activity is not accidental but reflects a world-wide general tendency which has already been described. Televiewing is a full evening's activity. Once the television set is switched on, most people find it difficult to switch it off again; and the couple sleeping in front of the switched-on television set is by now a standard element of jokes, and an everyday reality in many families.

This trend is stimulated and sustained by the actual form of an evening's telecast, which is in marked contrast to the printed schedule. There are hardly any "empty" interval points between the published programme items. The published schedule is intricately interwoven with "hidden" strands of another type of programme, which not only appear in the interval between the items but also at unannounced times within these items as well: commercials, TV internal publicity, and national symbols and messages. Appendices 8.1 and 8.2 attempt to present the emerging pattern for one day, but as static descriptions, they fall short of conveying the dynamic flux of the actual experience of viewing:

> What is being offered is not, in older terms, a programme of discrete units with particular insertions, but a planned flow in which the true series is not the published sequence of programme items but this sequence transformed by the inclusion of another kind of sequence, so that these sequence together compose the real flow, the real 'broadcasting'. (Williams 1974, p. 90.)

There are hardly any intervals in the traditional sense, and even the published times for the "Opening" and "Close" are not just points in time, between which the evening's telecast unfolds, but mark programme items in their own right.

There even seems to be a deliberate effort to further blur any distinguishing line between published and hidden programme items and hence hamper the immediate recognition of what kind of programme one is really watching. Contrary to previous practice in Singapore, there is today no signal marking the insertion of a commercial into a programme item. Advertisements often appear like a change of a film sequence, and one needs a second to realize whether the rising moon, or whatever appears on the screen, is part of the film or whether one has left the film story and the realm of fiction and is under the gentle persuasion to spend one's money in real Singapore. This constant oscillation between, for instance, the fictional high-class environment in "Magnum" and the same symbols of success offered for purchase in Singapore (such as expensive watches, bank connections, and all the smaller amenities of everyday life available to the prospering middle-class) gives a special colouring to Singapore's televiewing experience and makes it an inseparable and concordant part of everyday life experience.

This idea of an evening's televiewing as the usual form of television consumption is acknowledged by television planners and directly influences and guides the programming policy of SBC: the Annual Report states that "the desirability of a follow-through audience" is one of the factors taken into account when planning the TV programme transmission schedule (**SBC Annual**

Report 1980/81, p. 24). In line with these considerations, the internal announcements, which, with very few exceptions, give information only about the channel in which they appear, can be seen as a means to sustain the audience's interest to stay with that channel. The first chairman of SBC criticized the use of trailers as insufficient and suggested an increased promotion of television programmes via television (Ong Teng Cheong 1980).

A closer look at prime-time television programmes on the Wednesday, for which a detailed analysis is provided in Appendices 8.1 and 8.2, will show another aspect of the concept of flow in televiewing. Prime time, marked by an upward jump in the number of viewers, starts on weekdays between 7 and 8 p.m., and ends between 10 and 11 p.m. The analysis reveals a more intricate pattern of interweaving the published and hidden programme strands for Channel 8, compared to Channel 5. On both channels, however, prime time is taken up mainly by a succession of entertainment programmes, which brings the entertainment share on Channel 5 to almost the same high level of 70% as in Channel 8. This flow of entertainment is "interrupted" by the news and one educational/informational programme on each channel. While television news is usually not seen as an unwelcome interruption -- they attract about the same number of viewers as most entertainment programmes -- educational/informational programmes are apparently treated differently (at least when they appear in the context of entertainment programmes): audience data of SRS show a decline in the number of viewers for these programmes. On Channel 5, the opinion programme is shown so late (starting only after 10 p.m.) that one can expect a decrease in the number of viewers because of the time besides the fact that only a small number will be interested in this more demanding fare. The case of Channel 8 is different. Here the documentary is set in the middle of the evening's entertainment programme. SRS data show that at the time of that documentary (8.30 - 9.00 p.m.) there is a considerable decrease in the audience figure in the otherwise continuous high plateau stretching between 7 and 10 p.m. for Channel 8. In the case of Channel 5, which transmits a detective drama during that time, there is a somewhat corresponding increase. It seems arguable that this increase during the thirty-minute slot on Channel 5, is a consequence of the audience's idea that an evening's experience of television as entertainment should not be interrupted. This temporary switching of channels, then, could be explained as an indication that the television audience starts constructing its own "television flow" as soon as the smooth flow planned and offered by the broadcasting station is, in its view, interrupted or impeded.

APPENDICES

APPENDIX 1
Distribution of Programme Types by Air-time

Type of Programme		Air-time in Each Language (in minutes)				Total		Total Air-Time of Programme Type in	
		English	Chinese	Malay	Tamil	Hrs:Min	%	Hrs:Min	%
News		245	140	140	140	11:05		11:05	9.6
Documentary	Culture & Arts	165	15	35	–	3:35	29.3		
	Current Affairs	180	–	–	–	3:00	24.5		
	History	30	–	–	–	0:30	4.1		
	Magazine	40	35	–	–	1:15	10.2		
	Nature	95	25	25	25	2:50	23.1		
	Science	65	–	–	–	1:05	8.8		
	Total	575	75	60	25	12:15	100	12:15	10.7
Opinion		155	45	–	–	3:20		3:20	2.9
Education	Arts & Crafts	30	–	–	–	0:30			
	Physical Exercise	20	–	–	–	0:20			
	Road Safety	10	–	–	–	0:10			
	Sports	25	–	–	–	0:25			
	Women's Magazine	–	–	25	–	0:25			
	Total	85	–	25	–	1:50		1:50	1.6

APPENDIX I (Continued)
Distribution of Programme Types by Air-time

Type of Programme		Air-time in Each Language (in minutes)				Total		Total Air-Time of Programme Type in	
		English	Chinese	Malay	Tamil	Hrs:Min	%	Hrs:Min	%
Local Information	Culture & Entertainment	20	30	-	-	0:50		0:50	0.7
Children	Drama & Narration	520	100	-	50	11:10	67.3		
	Education & Information	275	25	25	-	5:25	32.7		
	Total	795	125	25	50	16:35	100	16:35	14.3
Drama	Adventure	970	335	-	-	21:45	42.0		
	Family & Society	705	850	80	140	29:35	57.0		
	Legends & Mythology	-	-	-	30	0:30	1.0		
	Total	1675	1185	80	170	51:50	100	51:50	44.8
Sports		220	-	-	-	3:40		3:40	3.2
Music		5	15	-	5	0:25		0:25	0.4
Show	Games & Quiz	-	60	-	-	1:00			
	Musical/Variety	395	210	90	55	12:30			
	Total	395	270	90	55	13:30		13:30	11.6
Commercial	Shopping Guide	10	10	-	-	0:20		0:20	0.2
Total	min	4180 =	1895 =	420 =	445 =	6940 =			
	hrs:min	69:40	31:35	7:00	7:25	115:40		115:40	100.0

APPENDIX 2

Programmes of the Week: Titles

Type		English	Chinese	Malay	Tamil
News (35)		News in Brief (7x)	News and Weather Forecast (7x)	News and Weather Forecast (7x)	News and Weather Forecast (7x)
		News and Weather Forecast (7x)			
Documentary (29)	Culture & Arts (8)	Around the World with Brian Adams	Musical Soiree (50$)	Rentak Tari	
		Artivity			
		The English Literature - The Victorian Period			
		Made by Hands - Blackwood			
		Patricia's Moving Image			
		That's Hollywood - Hollywood's Unsung Heroes			
		Musical Soiree (50$)			
	Current Affairs (5)	The Age of Uncertainty - Democracy, Leadership, Commitment			
		Focus - Problems of Economic Growth			
		Hong Kong - Sweat Shop or Sanitized Factory			
		Newsnight - Jerry Rawling			
		Newsweek - Germany: The Miracle Fades			
	History (1)	Journey Into Japan			
	Magazine (2)	You Asked for It	30-Minute Focus		

APPENDIX 2 (Continued)
Programmes of the Week: Titles

Type		English	Chinese	Malay	Tamil
	Nature (9)	Birds of the Sea The Human Body - Muscular System Living Tomorrow Sea-coasts Thacker's World Rocks and Minerals	Friends of Man - Reindeer	Expedition to the Animal Kingdom - In the Jungle of the Lion King	Wild Kingdom - The Cheetah Shall Survive
	Science (4)	Air Learning about Solar Energy Magazine Zero One Walter Cronkite's Universe			
Opinion (4)		Confucius' Philosophy (Lecture) Debate '82 Opinion: It's Your Life In Their Hands	Discussion on Confucianism		
Education (6)	Arts & Craft	Erica - Far Eastern Inspiration			
	Road Safety	Skills of Defensive Driving			
	Physical Exercise	Exercise with Gloria			
	Sports	Basketball for Girls - Funda- mental Techniques Tennis - The Nasty Way: The Serve and the Volley			

APPENDIX 2 (Continued)
Programmes of the Week: Titles

Type	English	Chinese	Malay	Tamil
Local Information (6)			Serikandi	
	Women's Magazine			
Culture & Entertainment	Cultural Diary (3x)	Cultural Diary (3x)		
Music (5)	Errol Buddle Jazz Band	World Music Album (3x)		Tabla
Sports (5)	Olympic Minutes Sports Special – The World Championship of Women's Golf World Cup Soccer '82 – USSR vs New Zealand World of Sports World Sportsman			
Show (14)				
Games & Quiz (1)		The Name of the Game		
Musical/Variety (13)	The Black and White Minstrel Show The 50's Connection In Person – Gigi Villa and Rudolph van der Ven Showtime Special – Liberace in Las Vegas Solid Gold Thursday Entertainment Special – Night of 100 Stars	Ode to the Night Sing, Sing, Sing 'Live' from Studio One (2x)	Muzikarama Temanika	Kalai Thiram '82

APPENDIX 2 (Continued)

Programmes of the Week: Titles

Type		English	Chinese	Malay	Tamil
Children's Programmes (44)	Drama & Narration (32)	ABC Children's Short Story Baldmoney, Sneezewort, Dodder and Cloudberry The Black Arrow - The Ambush The Book Bird - The TV Kid Children's Feature - Flash the Sheepdog A Horse in the House Kebekio in the Land of 'I Want' - The Three Little Pigs A Little Silver Trumpet Maggie's Moor Memoir of a Fairy Godmother Mother Goose Rhymes The Ravelled Thread - The Felon Secret Valley - The Trojan Bull Share a Story - Animal Bushes Share a Story - The Little Green Dragon A Tale of the Groundhog's Shadow The Whisper of Glocken			Story Time (2x)
	(Cartoons)	Barbapapa Curious George (2x) Flintstone Frolics Hans Christian Andersen - The Snow Queen Kimba - Jungle Justice Mr Magoo Spiderman Yogi's Gang	Gatchaman Heidi Misha World Famous Fairy Tales		

APPENDIX 2 (Continued)

Programmes of the Week: Titles

Type	English	Chinese	Malay	Tamil
Education & Information (12)	Dragons, Wagons and Wax The Electric Company Everyone's a Winner The Great Space Coaster Habits of Health - Keeping in Shape Kidsworld Make Merry with Music New Zoo Revue Sesame Street 3-2-1 Contact - Order Disorder	Dr Miao	Lima Sekawan	
Drama (53) Adventure (20)	The Chisholms - Endless Desert The Wonderful World of Disney - Treasure of Matecumbe	The Chivalrous Pugilist Dynasty (2x) On the Waterfront (2x)		
(Detective)	Cassie & Co - Dark Side of the Moon The Century Turns Chicago Story - Vendetta The Last Song McClain's Law - Requiem for a Narc Magnum - Tropical Madness The Private Life of Sherlock Holmes Shannon - A Favour for an Enemy Supertrain Target - Promises The Wild Wild West - The Night of the Spanish Curse	Shogun Samurai G-Men 75		

APPENDIX 2 (Continued)

Programmes of the Week: Titles

Type	English	Chinese	Malay	Tamil
Family & Social (32)	All Creatures Great and Small Cosmopolitan Theatre – The German Lesson Dallas – Vengeance East of Eden Falcon Crest – Heir Apparant Father Murphy – Will's Surprise The Flame Tree of Thika – A Real Sportsman The Misfits	Crocodile Tears Current Eleven Women – Last Summer A House Is not a Home The Jaws (2x) A Love Forever Our Beloved Daughter The Promise	Sandiwara – Belitan Sandiwara – Retak Retak Arca	Apnapan (Hindi Movie) General Chakravanthy (Tamil Movie)
(Comedy)	Benson Best of the West – The Calico Kid Goes to School Harper Valley, PTA Laverne and Shirley Love, Sydney – Welcome Home Mr Marlin – The Music's In Me Mork and Mindy – I've Got to Run One in a Million – The Committee The Paleface	Time for Wine and Roses Unforgettable Love		
Legends & Mythology (1)				Ramayana – Rama's Messenger

APPENDIX 3.1
Programme Types in Each Language: Proportion of Total Air-Time

Type	English	Chinese	Malay	Tamil	Total
News	3.6	2.0	2.0	2.0	9.6
Documentary	8.3	1.1	0.9	0.4	10.7
Opinion	2.3	0.6	-	-	2.9
Education	1.2	-	0.4	-	1.6
Local Information	0.3	0.4	-	-	0.7
Children's Programmes	11.4	1.9	0.3	0.7	14.3
Drama	24.1	17.1	1.2	2.4	44.8
Sports	3.2	-	-	-	3.2
Music	0.1	0.2	-	0.1	0.4
Show	5.6	3.9	1.3	0.8	11.6
Commercial	0.1	0.1	-	-	0.2
	60.2	27.3	6.1	6.4	100.0

APPENDIX 3.2
Programme Types: Proportion for Each Language

Type	English	Chinese	Malay	Tamil	Total Air-Time of Programme Type
News	5.9	7.4	33.3	31.5	9.6
Documentary	13.8	4.0	14.3	5.6	10.7
Opinion	3.7	2.4	-	-	2.9
Education	2.0	-	6.0	-	1.6
Local Information	0.5	1.6	-	-	0.7
Children's Programme	19.0	6.6	6.0	11.2	14.3
Drama	40.1	62.5	19.0	38.2	44.8
Sports	5.3	-	-	-	3.2
Music	0.1	0.8	-	1.1	0.4
Show	9.4	14.2	21.4	12.4	11.6
Commercial	0.2	0.5	-	-	0.2
	100.0	100.0	100.0	100.0	100.0

APPENDIX 4
Programmes with Subtitles

Type	Language Spoken	Subtitles	Title
Drama	Chinese	English	The Chivalrous Pugilist Crocodile Tears Current Dynasty (2x) G-Men 75 A House Is Not a Home The Jaws (2x) A Love Forever On the Waterfront (2x) Our Beloved Daughter The Promise Shogun Samurai
	Chinese	English/ Chinese/ Malay	Unforgettable Love Time for Wine and Roses
	English	Malay	Cassie & Co - Dark Side of the Moon Falcon Crest - Heir Apparent Father Murphy - Will's Surprise The Last Song McClain's Law - Requiem for a Narc Magnum - Tropical Madness Shannon - A Favour for an Enemy
	English	Chinese	Chicago Story - Vendetta The Misfits The Wonderful World of Disney - Treasure of Matecumbe
	Malay	English	Sandiwara - Belitan Sandiwara - Retak Retak Arca
	Hindi	English/ Malay	Apnapan

APPENDIX 4 (Continued)
Programmes with Subtitles

Type	Language Spoken	Subtitles	Title
	Tamil	English/Malay	General Chakravanthy
	Tamil	English	Ramayana - Rama's Messenger
Documentary	English	Chinese	Newsweek - Germany: The Miracle Fades Newsnight - Jerry Rawling Journey into Japan
	Chinese	English	Friends of Man - Reindeer
	Malay	English	Expedition to the Animal Kingdom - In the Jungle of the Lion King
	Tamil	English	Wild Kingdom - The Cheetah Shall Survive
Music	-	Chinese	World Music Album (3x)

APPENDIX 5.1
Imported Programmes: Types and Distribution

Country of Origin (Western)	Type of Programme	Number of Programmes	Air-Time (Hrs:Min)	% of Total Air-Time
United States	Documentary	12	4:10	3.6
	Education	5	1:25	1.2
	Children's Programme:			
	Educ./Inform.	9	4:20	3.7
	Others	12	3:15	2.8
	Drama	25	22:15	19.2
	Sports	3	1:15	1.1
	Show	4	4:55	4.3
	Total	70	41:35	35.9
United Kingdom	Documentary	4	2:15	2.0
	Children's Programme	8	3:45	3.3
	Drama	4	4:45	4.1
	Show	1	0:50	0.7
	Total	17	11:45	10.1
Germany	Documentary	4	1:05	0.9
	Drama	1	0:55	0.8
	Total	5	2:00	1.7
Canada	Documentary	3	1:15	1.1
	Children's Programme	1	0:15	0.2
	Total	4	1:30	1.3
Australia	Documentary	1	0:30	0.4
	Children's Programme	1	0:25	0.4
	Music	1	0:05	0.1
	Total	3	1:00	0.9
Spain	Sports	1	0:55	0.8
Netherlands	Children's Programme	1	0:05	0.1

APPENDIX 5.1 (Continued)
Imported Programmes: Types and Distribution

Country of Origin (Asian)	Type of Programme	Number of Programmes	Air-Time (Hrs:Min)	% of Total Air-Time
Hong Kong	Drama	10	12:15	10.6
Taiwan	Drama	5	5:10	4.5
	Show	1	0:45	0.6
	Total	6	5:55	5.1
Japan	Children's Programme	5	2:05	1.8
	Drama	3	2:20	2.0
	Music	3	0:15	0.2
	Total	11	4:40	4.0
India	Drama	2	2:20	2.0
Brunei	Education	1	0:25	0.4
Total		131	84:15	72.9

APPENDIX 5.2
Imported Programmes: Country of Origin

UNITED STATES (70 programmes)

Documentary (12)	Culture & Arts	Around the World with Brian Adams
		The English Literature - The Victorian Period
		That's Hollywood - Hollywood's Unsung Heroes
	Magazine	You Asked for It
	Nature	Birds of the Sea
		The Human Body - Muscular System
		Sea-coasts
		Thacker's World
		Wild Kingdom - The Cheetah Shall Survive
		Rocks and Minerals
	Science	Learning about Solar Energy
		Walter Cronkite's Universe

Education (5)	Arts & Craft	Erica - Far Eastern Inspiration
	Physical Exercise	Exercise with Gloria
	Road Safety	Skills of Defensive Driving
	Sports	Basketball for Girls - Fundamental Techniques
		Tennis - The Nasty Way: The Serve and the Volley

Children's Programme (21)	Drama & Narration	ABC Children's Short Story
		The Book Bird - The TV Kid
		Memoirs of a Fairy Godmother
		Mother Goose Rhymes
		A Tale of the Groundhog's Shadow
	(Cartoons)	Curious George (2x)
		Flintstone Frolics
		Hans Christian Andersen - The Snow Queen
		Mr Magoo
		Spiderman
		Yogi's Gang

APPENDIX 5.2 (Continued)
Imported Programmes: Country of Origin

UNITED STATES (70 programmes)

Children's Programme (21)	Education & Information	Dragons, Wagons, and Wax
		The Electric Company
		Everyone's a Winner
		The Great Space Coaster
		Habits of Health - Keeping in Shape
		Kidsworld
		New Zoo Revue
		Sesame Street
		3-2-1 Contact - Order Disorder

Drama	Adventure (11)	The Chisholms
		The Wonderful World of Disney - Treasure of Matecumbe
	(Detective)	Cassie & Co - Dark Side of the Moon
		The Century Turns
		Chicago Story
		The Last Song
		McClain's Law - Requiem for a Narc
		Magnum - Tropical Madness
		Shannon - A Favour for an Enemy
		Supertrain
		The Wild Wild West - The Night of the Spanish Curse
	Family & Social (14)	Dallas - Vengeance
		East of Eden
		Falcon Crest - Heir Apparent
		Father Murphy - Will's Surprise
		Harper Valley, PTA
		Love, Sydney - Welcome Home
		The Misfits
	(Comedy)	Benson
		Best of the West - The Calico Kid Goes to School
		Laverne and Shirley
		Mr Merlin - The Music's in Me
		Mork and Mindy - I've Got to Run
		One in a Million - The Committee
		The Paleface

APPENDIX 5.2 (Continued)
Imported Programmes: Country of Origin

UNITED STATES (70 programmes)

Sports (3)		Olympic Minutes
		Sports Special - The World Championship of Women's Golf
		World Sportsman
Show (4)	Musical	The 50's Connection
		Showtime Special - Liberace in Las Vegas
		Solid Gold
		Thursday Entertainment Special - Night of 100 Stars

UNITED KINGDOM (17 programmes)

Documentary (4)	Current Affairs	The Age of Uncertainty - Democracy, Leadership, Commitment
		Newsnight - Jerry Rawling
		Newsweek - Germany: The Miracle Fades
	Nature	Living Tomorrow
Children's Programme (8)	Drama & Narration	Baldmoney, Sneezewort, Dodder and Cloudberry
		The Black Arrow - The Ambush
		Children's Feature - Flash the Sheepdog
		A Horse in the House
		A Little Silver Trumpet
		Maggie's Moor
		The Ravelled Thread - The Felon
		The Whisper of Glocken
Drama (4)	Adventure (Detective)	The Private Life of Sherlock Holmes
		Target - Promises
	Family & Social	All Creatures Great and Small
		The Flame Tree of Thika - A Real Sportsman
Show	Musical	The Black and White Minstrel Show

APPENDIX 5.2 (Continued)
Imported Programmes: Country of Origin

CANADA (4 programmes)

Documentary	Culture & Arts	Made by Hands - Blackwood
		Patricia's Moving Image
	Nature	Friends of Man - Reindeer

| Children's Programme | Drama & Narration | Kebekio in the Land of 'I Want' - The Three Little Pigs |

AUSTRALIA (3 programmes)

| Documentary | History | Journey into Japan |

| Children's Programme | Drama & Narration | Secret Valley - The Trojan Bull |

| Music | | Errol Buddle Jazz Band |

GERMANY (5 programmes)

Documentary	Current Affairs	Focus - Problems of Economic Growth in the Third World
	Nature	Expedition to the Animal Kingdom - In the Jungle of the Lion King
	Science	Air Magazine Zero One

| Drama | Family & Social | Cosmopolitan Theatre - The German Lesson |

NETHERLANDS

| Children's Programme | Cartoon | Barbapapa |

APPENDIX 5.2 (Continued)
Imported Programmes: Country of Origin

SPAIN

Sports | | World Cup Soccer '82 -
 | | USSR vs New Zealand

HONG KONG (10 programmes)

Drama (10) | Adventure | Dynastic (2x)
 | | On the Waterfront (2x)
 | (Comedy) | Time for Wine and Roses
 | Family & | Crocodile Tears
 | Social | The Jaws (2x)
 | | A House Is Not A Home
 | | A Love Forever

TAIWAN (6 programmes)

Drama (5) | Adventure | The Chivalrous Pugilist
 | Family & Social | Current
 | | Eleven Women - Last Summer
 | | The Promise
 | | Unforgettable Love

Show | Musical | Ode to the Night

JAPAN (11 programmes)

Children's | Drama & | Gatchaman
Programme (5) | Narration | Heidi
 | (Cartoons) | Kimba - Jungle Justice
 | | Misha
 | | World Famous Fairy Tales

APPENDIX 5.2 (Continued)
Imported Programmes: Country of Origin

JAPAN (11 programmes)

Drama (3)	Adventure	Shogun Samurai
	(Detective)	G-Men 75
	Family & Social	Our Beloved Daughter

Music		World Music Album (3x)

INDIA

Drama	Family & Social	Apnapan (Hindi Movie)
		General Chakravanthy (Tamil Movie)

BRUNEI

Education	Women's Magazine	Serikandi

APPENDIX 5.3

SBC Productions and Imported Programmes as a Percentage of Total Air-Time

Type of Programme	Total Air-Time (Hrs:Min)	SBC Duration (Hrs:Min)	SBC % of Total Air-Time	Imported Duration (Hrs:Min)	Imported % of Total Air-Time
News	11:05	11:05	9.6	-	-
Documentary	12:15	3:00	2.6	9:15	8.1
Opinion	3:20	3:20	2.9	-	-
Education	1:50	-	-	1:50	1.6
Local Information	0:50	0:50	0.7	-	-
Children's Programme	16:35	2:25	2.1	14:10	12.2
Drama	51:50	1:50	1.6	50:00	43.2
Sports	3:40	1:30	1.3	2:10	1.9
Music	0:25	0:05	0.1	0:20	0.3
Show	13:30	7:00	6.0	6:30	5.6
Commercial	0:20	0:20	0.2	-	-
Total	115:40	31:25	27.1	84:15	72.9

APPENDIX 5.4
SBC Productions and Imported Programmes as a Percentage of Programme Type

Type of Programme	Total Air-Time (Hrs:Min)	SBC Duration (Hrs:Min)	SBC % of Air-Time of Programme Type	Imported Duration (Hrs:Min)	Imported % of Air-Time of Programme Type
News	11:05	11:05	100.0	-	-
Documentary	12:15	3:00	24.5	9:15	75.5
Opinion	3:20	3:20	100.0	-	-
Education	1:50	-	-	1:50	100.0
Local Information	0:50	0:50	100.0	-	-
Children's Programme	16:35	2:25	14.6	14:10	85.4
Drama	51:50	1:50	3.5	50:00	96.5
Sports	3:40	1:30	40.9	2:10	59.1
Music	0:25	0:05	20.0	0:20	80.0
Show	13:30	7:00	51.9	6:30	48.1
Commercial	0:20	0:20	100.0	-	-
Total	115:40	31:25		84.15	

APPENDIX 5.5
SBC Productions

Type		English	Min	Chinese	Min	Malay	Min	Tamil	Min
News		News in Brief (7x)	70	News & Weather Forecast (7x)	140	News & Weather Forecast (7x)	140	News & Weather Forecast (7x)	140
		News & Weather Forecast (7x)	175						
Documentary	Culture & Arts	Artivity	30						
		Musical Soiree (50$)	15	Musical Soiree (50$)	15	Rentak Tari	35		
	Current Affairs	Hong Kong - Sweat Shop or Sanitized Factory	50						
	Magazine			30-Minute Focus	35				
Opinion		Confucius' Philosophy: Development over the Ages by Prof Tu Wei-Ming	50	Discussion with Prof Hsu Cho-Yun & Dr Chin Chen Oi on Confucianism	45				
		Debate '82: 1st Quarter Final	60						
		Opinion: It's Your Life In Their Hands	45						
Education		-		-		-		-	

APPENDIX 5.5 (Continued)
SBC Productions

Type		English	Min	Chinese	Min	Malay	Min	Tamil	Min
Local Information	Culture & Entertainment	Cultural Diary (3x)	20	Cultural Diary (3x)	30				
Children's Programme	Drama & Narration	Share A Story: The Little Green Dragon Share a Story: Animal Bushes	10 10					Story Time (2x)	50
	Education & Information	Make Merry with Music	25	Dr Miao	25	Lima Sekawan	25		
Drama	Family & Social					Sandiwara: Belitan Sandiwara: Retak Retak Arca	40 40		
	Legends & Mythology							Ramayana: Rama's Messenger (Part VI)	30
Sports		World of Sports	90						

APPENDIX 5.5 (Continued)
SBC Productions

Type		English	Min	Chinese	Min	Malay	Min	Tamil	Min
Music								Tabla	5
Show	Games & Quiz			The Name of the Game	60				
	Musical	In Person: Gigi Villa & Rudolph van der Ven	50	Sing, Sing, Sing	50	Muzikarama	45	Kalai Thiram '82	55
	Variety			'Live' from Studio I (2x)	115	Temanika	45		
Commercial		Your Shopping Guide	10	Your Shopping Guide	10				

APPENDIX 6
Commercials

Figures in this category are only a close approximation to the real telecast, since on four days the necessary change of cassettes was made during a commercial interval between programmes. The data for these days have been compensated by averaging the number and type of the same commercial interval on the remaining three days. Since no far-reaching conclusions are based on the exact number of commercials in the different groups, this decision seems justifiable, especially since the length of the individual advertisement is not taken into account in the following listing. As the length of individual items differs from about 20 to about 60 seconds, this would change the picture again.

Channel 5 : 542 advertisements = 4:16 hours = 5.9% air-time in the Channel
Channel 8 : 427 advertisements = 4:26 hours = 10.4% air-time in the Channel

Total : 969 advertisements = 8:42 hours = 7.5% of total air-time

Product/Service Advertised	Number of Ads	Percentage
1. Food/sweets/non-alcoholic drinks	239	24.6
2. Cosmetics/personal hygiene products	189	19.5
3. Watches	73	7.5
4. Alcoholic drinks	69	7.1
5. Other household products	61	6.3
6. Cleaning/washing products	44	4.5
7. (a) Banks/insurance/credit cards	36	3.7
(b) Clothes/shoes	36	3.7
8. Cars + accessories	31	3.2
9. Shops	29	3.0
10. Health/medicine	28	2.9
11. Restaurants	23	2.4
12. (a) TV/radios	19	2.0
(b) Events/exhibitions	19	2.0
13. Cinema/light literature	16	1.7
14. Miscellaneous	57	5.9
Total	969	100

APPENDIX 7.1
Programmes Telecast on Monday, 13 September 1982

CHANNEL 5

Time	Language Spoken	Language Subtitled	Type	Title
3.00	C	E	Drama	(Opening) On the Waterfront
3.45	E		Documentary	Rocks and Minerals
4.05	T		Children	Story Time
4.30	E		Drama	One in a Million - The Committe
4.55	E		Education	Erica - Far Eastern Inspiration
5.25	E		Children	The Great Space Coaster
5.50	E		Children	A Horse in the House
6.15	E		News	News
6.25	E		Documentary	Walter Cronkite's Universe
6.55	E		Children	Barbapapa
7.00	E		Children	Spiderman
7.30	M		News	News and Weather Forecast
7.50	M		Show	Muzikarama
8.35	E		Documentary	Magazine Zero One
8.45	E	M	Drama	McClain's Law - Requiem for a Narc
9.45	E		News	News and Weather Forecast
10.10	E		Show	Solid Gold
11.10	E		Drama	East of Eden
12.00				(Close)

CHANNEL 8

Time	Language Spoken	Language Subtitled	Type	Title
6.00	E		Children	(Opening) Baldmoney, Sneezewort, Dodder and Cloudberry
6.20	T	E	Documentary	Wild Kingdom - The Cheetah Shall Survive
6.45	T		News	News and Weather Forecast
7.05	E		Documentary	Patricia's Moving Image
7.30	C	E	Drama	The Promise
8.05	C		Show	'Live' from Studio 1
9.00	C		News	News and Weather Forecast
9.20	C		Opinion	Discussion on Confucianism
10.05	C	E	Drama	Shogun Samurai
10.50	E		Drama	Harper Valley, PTA
11.15				(Close)

APPENDIX 7.2
Programmes Telecast on Tuesday, 21 September 1982

CHANNEL 5

Time	Language Spoken	Subtitled	Type	Title
3.00	C	E	Drama	(Opening) Crocodile Tears
4.30	E		Drama	The Century Turns
6.05	E		Documentary	Learning about Solar Energy
6.15	E		News	News
6.25	M		Education	Serikandi
6.50	E		Children	Mr Magoo
6.55	E		Children	Yogi's Gang
7.20	E		Children	Share a Story - The Little Green Dragon
7.30	M		News	News and Weather Forecast
7.50	E		Show	In Person - Gigi Villa and Rudolph Van Der Ven
8.40	E	M	Drama	Father Murphy - Will's Surprise
9.45	E		News	News and Weather Forecast
10.10	E		Local Inform.	Cultural Diary
10.15	E		Documentary	Newsweek - Germany: The Miracle Fades
10.50	E		Documentary	Newsnight - Jerry Rawling
11.15	E		Drama	Target - Promises
12.10				(Close)

CHANNEL 8

Time	Language Spoken	Subtitled	Type	Title
6.00	E		Children	The Whisper of Glocken
6.15	T		Music	Tabla
6.20	T		Children	Story Time
6.45	T		News	News and Weather Forecast
7.05	C		Children	Dr Miau
7.30	E		Children	A Tale of the Groundhog's Shadow
7.40	E		Documentary	Artivity
8.10	C	E	Drama	Our Beloved Daughter
9.00	C		News	News and Weather Forecast
9.20	C		Commercial	Your Shopping Guide
9.30	C	E	Drama	Dynasty
10.25	E		Drama	Love, Sydney - Welcome Home
10.55				(Close)

APPENDIX 7.3
Programmes Telecast on Wednesday, 22 September 1982

CHANNEL 5

Time	Language Spoken	Subtitled	Type	Title
3.00	C	E	Drama	(Opening) The Jaws
4.35	E		Education	Exercise with Gloria
4.55	E		Documentary	Thacker's World
5.20	E		Children	The Electric Company
5.50	E		Children	Maggie's Moor
6.15	E		News	News
6.25	E		Documentary	Around the World with Brian Adam
6.55	E		Children	Curious George
7.00	E		Drama	Benson
7.30	M		News	News and Weather Forecast
7.50	M	E	Drama	Sandiwara - Belitan
8.30	E		Commercial	Your Shopping Guide
8.40	E	M	Drama	Magnum - Tropical Madness
9.45	E		News	News and Weather Forecast
10.10	E		Opinion	Confucius' Philosophy - Development over the Ages
11.00	E		Show	The 50's Connection
11.40	E		Drama	Laverne and Shirley
12.05				(Close)

CHANNEL 8

Time	Language Spoken	Subtitled	Type	Title
6.00	E		Children	(Opening) The Book Bird - The TV Kid
6.20	E		Children	Kimba - Jungle Justice
6.45	T		News	News and Weather Forecast
7.05	T	E	Drama	Ramayana - Rama's Messenger
7.35	C		Show	The Name of the Game
8.35	C	E	Documentary	Friends of Man - Reindeer
9.00	C		News	News and Weather Forecast
9.20		C	Music	World Music Album - P Tchaikovsky
9.25	C		Local Inform.	Cultural Diary
9.35	C	E	Drama	A Love Forever
10.55				(Close)

APPENDIX 7.4
Programmes Telecast on Thursday, 16 September 1982

CHANNEL 5

Time	Language Spoken	Subtitled	Type	Title
3.00	C	E	Drama	(Opening) Dynasty
3.50	E		Children	Curious George
3.55	E		Drama	The Wild Wild West - The Night of the Spanish Curse
4.45	M	E	Documentary	Expedition to the Animal Kingdom - In the Jungle of the Lion King
5.10	E		Children	Kidsworld
5.30	E		Children	Everyone's a Winner
5.50	E		Children	Secret Valley - The Trojan Bull
6.15	E		News	News
6.25	E		Local Inform.	Cultural Diary
6.30	E		Documentary	You Asked For It
7.10	E		Documentary	Seacoasts
7.20	E		Children	Share a Story - Animal Bushes
7.30	M		News	News and Weather Forecast
7.50	E	M	Drama	The Last Song
8.50	E		Drama	Supertrain
9.45	E		News	News and Weather Forecast
10.10	E		Show	Thursday Night Entertainment Special - Night of the 100 Stars
12.35				(Close)

CHANNEL 8

Time	Language Spoken	Subtitled	Type	Title
6.00	E		Children	Dragons, Wagons, and Wax
6.20	E		Children	Memoir of a Fairy Godmother
6.45	T		News	News and Weather Forecast
7.05	E		Opinion	Debate '82
8.05	E		Documentary	The Human Body - Muscular System
8.15	C		Show	Ode to the Night
9.00	C		News	News and Weather Forecast
9.20		C	Music	World Music Album - R Wagner
9.25	C	E	Drama	On the Waterfront
10.15	Hindi	E+M	Drama	Apnapan
11.25				(Close)

APPENDIX 7.5
Programmes Telecast on Friday, 10 September 1982

CHANNEL 5

Time	Language Spoken	Subtitled	Type	Title
3.00	C	C,E,M	Drama	(Opening) Time for Wine and Roses
4.30	E		Sports	World Sportsman
5.00	E		Documentary	Made by Hand - Blackwood
5.25	E		Children	New Zoo Revue
5.50	E		Children	Ravelled Thread - The Felon
6.15	E		News	News
6.25	M		Documentary	Rentak Tari
7.00	E		Children	A Little Silver Trumpet
7.30	M		News	News and Weather Forecast
7.50	E		Opinion	Opinion - It's Your Life in Their Hands
8.35	E		Sports	Olympic Minutes
8.45	E	M	Drama	Shannon - A Favour for an Enemy
9.45	E		News	News and Weather Forecast
10.10	E	C	Drama	Chicago Story - Vendetta
11.20	E		Drama	Best of the West - Calico Kid Goes to School
11.50				(Close)

CHANNEL 8

Time	Language Spoken	Subtitled	Type	Title
6.05	E		Children	(Opening) Kebekio in the Land of 'I Want' - The Three Little Pigs
6.20	C		Children	Gatchaman
6.45	T		News	News and Weather Forecast
7.05	C	E	Drama	The Chivalrous Pugilist
7.50	C		Local Inform.	Cultural Diary
8.00	C		Show	'Live' from Studio 1
9.00	C		News	News and Weather Forecast
9.20		C	Music	World Music Album - E Waldteufel
9.25	C	E	Drama	Current
10.15	T	E,M	Drama	General Chakravanthy
11.25				(Close)

60

APPENDIX 7.6
Programmes Telecast on Saturday, 25 September 1982

CHANNEL 5

Time	Language Spoken	Subtitled	Type	Title
1.00	E		Children	(Opening) Sesame Street
2.05	E		Drama	The Private Life of Sherlock Holmes
4.10	E		Sports	World Cup Soccer '82 – USSR vs New Zealand
5.05	M		Show	Temanika
5.50	E		Children	Flintstone Frolics
6.15	E		News	News
6.25	E		Documentary	The English Literature – The Victorian Period
6.40	E		Drama	The Chisholms – Endless Desert
7.25	E		Music	Errol Buddle Jazz Band
7.30	M		News	News and Weather Forecast
7.50	E		Show	The Black and White Minstrel Show
8.40	E	M	Drama	Cassie & Co – Dark Side of the Moon
9.35	E		Local Inform.	Cultural Diary
9.45	E		News	News and Weather Forecast
10.10	E		Drama	Dallas – Vengeance
11.10	E	C	Drama	The Misfits
1.20				(Close)

APPENDIX 7.6 (Continued)
Programmes Telecast on Saturday, 25 September 1982

CHANNEL 8

Time	Language Spoken	Language Subtitled	Type	Title
2.45	E		Children	(Opening) Make Merry with Music - Let's Make Music
3.10	E		Children	3-2-1 Contact - Order Disorder
3.40	C		Children	Heidi
4.05	E		Drama	The Flame Trees of Thika - A Real Sportsman
4.55	E		Documentary	The Age of Uncertainty - Democracy, Leadership, Commitment
5.50	T		Show	Kalai Thiram '82
6.45	T		News	News and Weather Forecast
7.05	E		Documentary	Air
7.20	E		Education	Basketball for Girls - Fundamental Techniques
7.30	C	E	Drama	The Jaws
9.00	C		News	News and Weather Forecast
9.20	C		Documentary	30-Minute Focus
9.55	C	E,C,M	Drama	Unforgettable Love
11.40				(Close)

APPENDIX 7.7
Programmes Telecast on Sunday, 19 September 1982

CHANNEL 5

Time	Language Spoken	Subtitled	Type	Title
9.00	E		Children	(Opening) Children's Feature – Flash the Sheepdog
10.00	E		Children	Hans Christian Andersen Fairy Tales – The Snow Queen
10.25	M		Children	Lima Sekawan
10.50	E	C	Drama	The Wonderful World of Disney – Treasure of Matecumbe
11.35	E		Sports	World of Sports
1.05	E		Drama	Mork and Mindy – I've Got to Run
1.35	E		Drama	Mr Merlin – The Music's in Me
2.00	E	C	Documentary	Journey into Japan
2.30	E		Documentary	That's Hollywood – Hollywood's Unsung Heroes
2.55	E		Documentary	Birds of the Sea
3.05	E		Drama	The Paleface
4.45	M	E	Drama	Sandiwara – Retak Retak Arca
5.25	E		Documentary	Hong Kong – Sweat Shop or Sanitized Factory
6.15	E		News	News
6.25	E		Education	Skills of Defensive Driving
6.35	E		Drama	All Creatures Great and Small
7.30	M		News	News and Weather Forecast
7.50	E		Show	Showtime Special – Liberace
8.40	E		Education	Tennis: The Nasty Way – The Serve and the Volley
8.55	E	M	Drama	Falcon Crest – Heir Apparent
9.45	E		News	News and Weather Forecast
10.10	E		Drama	Cosmopolitan Theatre – The German Lesson
11.05	E		Sports	Sports Special – The World Championship of Women's Golf
11.40	E		Documentary	Focus
11.55				(Close)

63

APPENDIX 7.7 (Continued)
Programmes Telecast on Sunday, 19 September 1982

CHANNEL 8

Time	Language Spoken	Language Subtitled	Type	Title
3.00	C		Children	Misha
3.30	C		Drama	Eleven Women - Last Summer
4.45	C		Children	World Famous Fairy Tales
5.05	E		Children	Habits of Health - Keeping in Shape
5.20	E		Children	The Black Arrow - The Ambush
5.45	E		Children	ABC Children's Short Story - Mayday! Mayday!
6.05	E		Children	Mother Goose Rhymes
6.15	E,C		Documentary	Musical Soiree
6.45	T		News	News and Weather Forecast
7.05	C		Show	Sing, Sing, Sing
7.55	C	E	Drama	G-Men 75
8.40	E		Documentary	Living Tomorrow
9.00	C		News	News and Weather Forecast
9.20	C		Local Inform.	Cultural Diary
9.30	C	E	Drama	A House Is Not a Home
11.05	C			(Close)

APPENDIX 8.1
The Telecast Programme on Wednesday, 22 September 1982, Channel 5

(The length of the line marking the published items is not proportional to the duration of the item)

	Commercial (1)
3.00	OPENING National Anthem with shots from National Day Parade SBC: Welcome
	Commercial (1)
	THE JAWS 1 interruption: commercial (4)
4.35	EXERCISE WITH GLORIA
4.55	THACKER'S WORLD
	Commercial (1)
5.20	THE ELECTRIC COMPANY
5.50	MAGGIE'S MOOR
	SBC: 1 announcement "Tonight's Programme" - Board
	National Symbols: 3 photos of modern Singapore
	Commercial (1)
6.15	NEWS
	SBC: 2 advance announcements (a) "Opinion", (b) "Debate '82"
6.25	AROUND THE WORLD WITH BRIAN ADAMS
6.55	CURIOUS GEORGE
	National Campaign: "Road Safety"
	SBC: 2 advance announcements (a) "Battle Star Galactica" (b) "Road Show"

APPENDIX 8.1 (Continued)
The Telecast Programme on Wednesday, 22 September 1982, Channel 5

		Commercial (9)
7.00		BENSON
		1 interruption: Commercial (8)
		SBC: 1 announcement "Tonight's Programme" – Board
		National Symbols: 2 drawings of traditional Singapore
		SBC: 1 announcement "Invitation for Story-writing and Singing Competition" (filmlet)
		Commercial (1)
7.30		NEWS AND WEATHER FORECAST
7.50		SANDIWARA: BELITAN
8.30		YOUR SHOPPING GUIDE
		Commercial (9)
8.40		MAGNUM: TROPICAL MADNESS
		3 interruptions: commercial (8)
		commercial (8)
		commercial (7)
		SBC: 1 announcement "Tonight's Programme" – Board
		National Symbols: 2 drawings of traditional Singapore
		Commercial (12)
9.45		NEWS AND WEATHER FORECAST
		Commercial (1)
10.10		CONFUCIUS' PHILOSOPHY (LECTURE)
		SBC: 1 advance announcement "Confucian Ethics" – Lecture

APPENDIX 8.1 (Continued)
The Telecast Programme on Wednesday, 22 September 1982, Channel 5

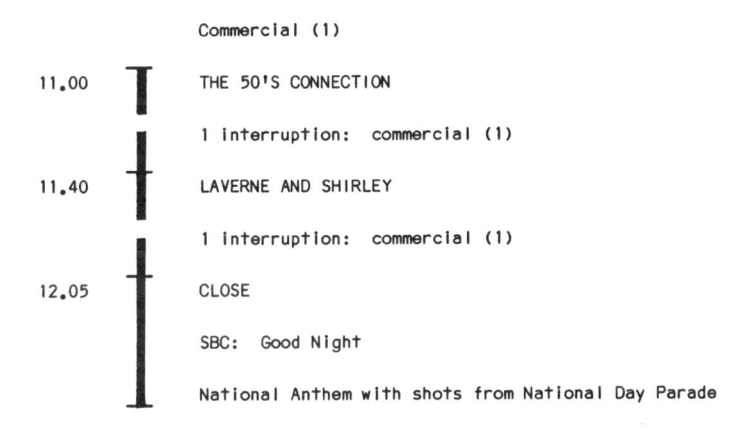

		Commercial (1)
11.00		THE 50'S CONNECTION
		1 interruption: commercial (1)
11.40		LAVERNE AND SHIRLEY
		1 interruption: commercial (1)
12.05		CLOSE
		SBC: Good Night
		National Anthem with shots from National Day Parade

APPENDIX 8.2
The Telecast Programme on Wednesday, 22 September 1982, Channel 8

(The length of the line marking the published items is not proportional to the duration of the item)

```
                    Commercial (1)
6.00        ┬       OPENING
            │       National Anthem with shots from National Day Parade
            │       SBC: Welcome
            ┴       Commercial (1)

            ┬       THE BOOK BIRD
            ┴       National Campaign: "Speak Mandarin"

6.20        ┬       KIMBA
            ┴       1 interruption: commercial (3)

                    SBC: 3 announcements (a) advance "Road Show", (b) "Tonight's
                         Programme" - Board, (c) "Radio Programme" - Board

                    National Symbols: 3 paintings of traditional Singapore

                    Commercial (1)

6.45        ┬       NEWS AND WEATHER FORECAST
            ┴       National Campaign: "Road Safety"

7.05        ┬       RAMAYANA
            ┴       Commercial (5)

7.35        ┬       THE NAME OF THE GAME
            │       3 interruptions:  commercial (8)
            │                         commercial (8)
            ┴                         commercial (8)
```

68

APPENDIX 8.2 (Continued)

The Telecast Programme on Wednesday, 22 September 1982, Channel 8

8.35 — FRIENDS OF MAN: REINDEER

SBC: 2 advance announcements: (a) "Chinese Opera", (b) "Tomorrow Night's Programme"

Commercial (4)

SBC: 1 advance announcement "Focus"

Commercial (5)

9.00 — NEWS AND WEATHER FORECAST

SBC: 2 advance announcements: (a) "Shopping Guide", (b) "Confucian Talk"

9.20 — WORLD MUSIC ALBUM

9.25 — CULTURAL DIARY

Commercial (10)

9.35 — A LOVE FOREVER

5 interruptions: commercial (6)
commercial (6)
commercial (6)
commercial (6)
commercial (6)

10.55 — CLOSE

SBC: Good Night

National Anthem with shots from National Day Parade

BIBLIOGRAPHY

Benjamin, G. "The Cultural Logic of Singapore's 'Multi-racialism'". In **Singapore: Society in Transition**, edited by R. Hassan, pp. 115-33. Kuala Lumpur: Oxford University Press, 1976.

Chan Heng Chee and H.D. Evers. "Nation-Building and National Identity in Southeast Asia". In **Building States and Nations - Vol. II: Analyses by Region**, edited by S.N. Eisenstadt and S. Rokkan, pp. 301-19. Beverly Hills, Ca.: Sage 1973.

Chen P.S.J. and Kuo E.C.Y. **Mass Media and Communication Patterns in Singapore.** Singapore: Amic, 1978.

Cheng Tong Fatt. "Corporation Structure in Singapore". In **Combroad**, pp. 6-9. December 1980.

Chew, S., "The Language of Survival". In **Singapore: Society in Transition,** edited by R. Hassan, pp. 149-54. Kuala Lumpur: Oxford University Press, 1976.

Clammer, J., "Modernization and Cultural Values: The Paradoxes of Transition in Singapore". In **Cultural Heritage versus Technological Development,** edited by R.E. Vente et al., pp. 223-40. Singapore: Maruzen Asia, 1981.

Hassan, R., "Symptoms and Syndrome of the Development Process". In **Singapore: Society in Transition**, edited by R. Hassan, pp. 339-47. Kuala Lumpur: Oxford University Press 1976.

Holsti, O.R., **Content Analysis for the Social Sciences and Humanities.** Reading, Mass.: Addison-Wesley, 1969.

Jones, R.L., and R.E. Carter. "Some Procedures for Estimating 'News Holes' in Content Analysis". In **Public Opinion**

Quarterly 3 (1959): 399-403.

Koh Tai Ann. "The Singapore Experience: Cultural Development in the Global Village". In **Southeast Asian Affairs 1980,** pp. 292-307. Singapore: Heinemann Asia for Institute of Southeast Asian Studies, 1980.

Ong Teng Cheong. "SBC: Changes for the Better" (Interview). In **The Mirror** 5 (1980): 1-4.

Ow Chin Hock. "Broadcasting in Singapore". In **People's Action Party 1954-1979** (Petir 25th Anniversary Issue). Singapore: PAP, 1979.

Singapore Broadcasting Corporation. **Annual Report 1980/81.** Singapore, n.d.

_____. **Annual Report 1981/1982.** Singapore, n.d.

Sitaram K.S., and L.W. Haapanen. "The Role of Values in Intercultural Communication". In **Handbook of Intercultural Communication,** edited by M.K. Asante et al., pp. 147-60. Beverly Hills, Ca.: Sage, 1979.

Survey Research Singapore. **Media Index: General Report.** Singapore, 1982.

_____. **Media Index: TV Rating Supplement, 1982/6** (Sunday 13 August 1982 - Saturday 25 September 1982).

Williams, R. **Television - Technology and Cultural Form.** London: Fontana Books, 1974.

HE 8700 .9 .S55 H45

THE AUTH

ERHARD U. HEIDT, Dr. rer. soc., is currently Reader in Education and Mass Communication at the University of Bielefeld, Federal Republic of Germany. He is also a consultant for UNESCO in the fields of media and educational technology and has written extensively on these topics. His monographs include **Instructional Media and the Individual Learner** (London and New York, 1978) and **Self-evaluation in Learning** (Paris: UNESCO, 1979).